DOGS
Photo-Fact Collection

Scientific Consultant
Diane Kelly
Ph.D., Zoology

Copyright © 2012, 2013 Kidsbooks, LLC
3535 West Peterson Avenue
Chicago, IL 60659

Printed in China
101302001SZ

Visit us at www.kidsbooks.com

Siberian Husky

CONTENTS

All About Dogs

Throughout history, dogs have been admired and loved by many people for their unique traits and behavior. They fetch balls, lick faces, and wag their tails with joy. Dogs also play with humans, hunt for sport, and herd animals.

Sniff, Sniff

A dog's sense of smell is nearly a million times better than ours! The secret lies mainly in the shape and size of the interior of a dog's nose, which contains a tremendous number of nerve endings and odor-sensing cells.

Weimaraner

6

Do you hear that? You didn't, but perhaps your dog did. Dogs can hear many sounds that are too high-pitched for humans to hear.

Pack of wolves

Family Matters

Dogs are descended from wolves, which are part of the same family as coyotes, jackals, and foxes. In the wild, these canids live and hunt in small groups and show powerful loyalty to their leader.

Play Time

When a dog's belly is close to the ground, and its rear end is raised, this behavior means it's time for fun.

Long Haired Chihuahua

English Bulldog

Getting Together

Dogs and humans have lived side by side for more than 15,000 years. Most likely, this relationship began when wild dogs started looking for food near human settlements. As the animals grew tamer, people started to keep them as pets. Dogs are considered to be "man's best friend," because they provide great companionship.

Getting the Point

Dogs have developed the ability to understand human gestures. If a person points at something, a dog will look where the person is pointing. Other animals, including chimpanzees, will just look at the person's finger.

German Shepherd

CUSTOM-BUILT Canines

Most modern dog breeds are less than 500 years old, but they come in an incredible range of shapes and sizes. The massive Saint Bernard can tip the scales at 200 pounds or more, while a tiny Pomeranian might weigh as little as 3 pounds.

Ready to Fight

Humans began breeding dogs to emphasize special traits and talents. For example, the Shar-Pei has loose, wrinkled skin, making it a hard-to-catch guard and fighting dog.

Pomeranian

Saint Bernard

On the Hunt

Centuries ago, dogs skilled in hunting were a huge asset to humans who lived as hunter-gatherers. Hunting breeds are still prized today for their special skills and unique temperaments. Known for their intelligence and alertness, Chesapeake Bay Retrievers make excellent duck hunters.

SETTERS

Setters were originally trained to crouch down in front of game birds, so that hunters could trap the birds with nets. Later, they learned to point. The Irish Setter has a thick coat that allows it to follow a trail through shrubs and thorns.

Doggy Paddle

It's no wonder Labrador Retrievers are great swimmers. Originally, they were trained to retrieve fishing nets through the icy waters off the coast of Newfoundland.

Point the Way

The classic Pointer was bred in England, Spain, and eastern Europe during the 17th century. Its name is derived from the way the dog stands motionless when it spots its game, pointing directly at it.

German Shorthaired Pointer

Herding Dogs

For more than 9,000 years, dogs have held jobs as sheep and cattle herders. The key to training a herder is to manage the dog's natural desire to hunt. Good herders stalk their charges and may even nip at them, but they never attack. For example, the Border Collie is so intelligent that it can carry out dozens of different commands.

Seeing the Light

Old English Sheepdogs peer at the world through a curtain of hair. It doesn't cramp their style, though. Dogs rely on smell and hearing much more than sight. And hair is good protection for the eyes when scurrying sheep kick up clouds of dust.

Leader of the Pack

The Australian Cattle Dog was bred to be the perfect herder. Since the 1800s, this dog has been known for its stamina and faithfulness.

INSTANT ID

One of the most unusual-looking dogs in the canine kingdom, the Puli has a soft, woolly undercoat and a long, coarse outercoat. Every Puli is a natural shepherd, and instinctively knows how to herd a flock of sheep or livestock.

Working Dogs

Dogs' loyalty, courage, and special talents make them perfect for jobs that improve people's lives. The German Shepherd's strength and intelligence has made it the first choice of police departments and the military. From trailing suspects to detecting explosives, German Shepherds adapt to a wide range of behaviors, making them superior working dogs.

FIRE!

Also known as firehouse dogs, Dalmatians have been hanging out with firefighters since the days of horse-drawn fire engines.

Giddy Up, Doggy!

Sled drivers use a few clear commands to control Siberian Huskies—such as "gee" (turn right), "haw" (turn left), "line out" (straighten up before moving), and "hike!" (Let's go!).

Lend a Hand

Labrador Retrievers make wonderful companions for people with physical disabilities. Specially trained from the time they are puppies, they fetch fallen objects, open doors, and bring food from cabinets.

15

Terrific Terriers

Hungry rodents have been plaguing farmers for countless centuries by invading their barns and eating valuable grain. Farmers fought back by breeding terriers, small dogs with powerful jaws that could slip into narrow spaces and ferret out the invaders. The Cairn Terrier is an animated and hardy little dog, with a fox-like expression.

Super Speedy

The Bedlington Terrier may look like a little lamb, but don't be fooled. These terriers are especially active. They are built for speed.

Canine Courage

Terriers are famous for never backing down, and many experts feel that the long-legged Airedale is, for its size, the world's most courageous dog.

BIG BULLY

The Boston Terrier was originally bred for dog fighting. At that time, these miniature dogs were called American Bull Terriers. Now that the "sport" is outlawed, Bull Terriers are recognized as separate breeds.

Boston Terrier

Staffordshire Bull Terrier

KING of DOGS

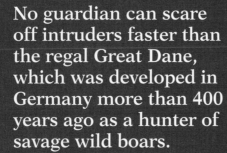

No guardian can scare off intruders faster than the regal Great Dane, which was developed in Germany more than 400 years ago as a hunter of savage wild boars.

War & Peace

Bulldogs were originally designed as fighting dogs. Over the centuries, the aggressive qualities have been bred out of them, but their courage and devotion are still there.

Rottweiler

English Bulldog

Beware of Dog

Dogs have been guarding the homes of their masters for centuries. A wall decoration uncovered in the ruins of Pompeii, an ancient Italian city, shows a fierce-looking dog with its teeth bared—beneath this scary image are the Latin words "*cave canem*" (beware the dog).

Some of the most popular watch dogs are the Rottweiler and the Doberman Pinscher. Rottweilers were used to herd cattle and Doberman Pinschers were once used as police dogs.

Doberman Pinscher

Comrade in Arms

In ancient Britain, Mastiffs fought side by side with their masters against Julius Caesar's Roman warriors. Centuries later, when the English knight Sir Peers Legh was wounded at the Battle of Agincourt, his loyal Mastiff defended him for hours until help arrived.

Toy Story

At the small end of the scale are the toy dogs, bred originally as house (or castle) pets for kings, queens, and nobles. The idea was to produce dogs that could easily be carried from place to place and cradled on laps.

Pugs were originally pets of Buddhist monks in Tibet. After being imported to Europe, the Pug became the favorite dog of England's King William II, who believed that a Pug had saved his life on the battlefield.

Butterfly Dog

The Papillon gets its name from its elegant ears, which resemble butterfly wings.

Soul Mate

The Chihuahua, which rarely weighs more than six pounds, can be traced back to the Aztecs of ancient Mexico. The Aztecs buried Chihuahuas with the dead, believing that the tiny dogs had the power to safely guide human souls through the underworld.

Little Lion

Shih Tzu means "lion" in Chinese, but these dogs, whose weight barely reaches double figures, are sweet-tempered and docile.

Cute and Cuddly

Toy Poodles come in a variety of colors, including black, white, blue, gray, beige, and apricot. Poodles are among the smartest of dogs, and make lovable pets.

Designer Dogs

Although purebred dogs make very good pets, mixed breeds are also excellent companions. Mongrels, or mutts, combine the characteristics of more than one breed. Most mutts are bred accidentally, but some breeders deliberately combine two breeds to create "designer dogs." For instance, the Labradoodle (half Labrador Retriever, half poodle) was first created in the 1970s for a blind woman whose husband was allergic to dogs.

Happy Dog

Loving and outgoing, Cockapoos are the cross-breed result of the friendly Cocker Spaniel and the low-shedding poodle. They interact well with people, even strangers and young children.

Healthier Cross?

Purebred dogs can inherit health problems. For example, a Pug's flat face may give it breathing problems. By crossing Pugs and Beagles to create Puggles, breeders hoped to make a healthier family pet that still had the Pug's wrinkly forehead.

BUYER BEWARE

There are more than 400 kinds of designer dogs, and more new types are created every year. Breeders of these dogs hope that their puppies will inherit the best qualities of each parent's breed, but it is possible that they will get undesirable traits from each breed instead. Chiweenies, a blend of the Chihuahua and the Dachshund, may develop knee problems due to their build.

Chiweenie

23

Flying High

Did you know that throwing a toy for your dog can be a competitive sport? At disc dog events, human-dog teams vie for prizes in distance, accuracy, and speed. Champion dogs jump high to catch their partner's throws!

Jack Russell Terrier

Good, Better, Best

At dog shows, male and female dogs are judged separately and prizes are awarded in many different categories. In the largest shows, judges may examine as many as 4,000 animals to select the best of each breed, the best of the seven major competitions, and finally, the best of the show.

Boxer

BEST OF BREED/VARIETY

KENNEL CLUB, INC.

Show Time

Some people love to train their dogs and take them to events to let them strut their stuff. Crufts, named after founder Charles Cruft, is one of the largest annual dog shows in the world. In the agility competition, dogs follow their owner's commands to race through a timed obstacle course.

Shetland Sheepdog

They are Off!

At top speeds over 40 miles an hour, greyhounds are the fastest dogs on Earth. Some Greyhounds are raced as sport in Greyhound racing, though this practice is controversial.

Puppy Love

From birth to 12 weeks old, puppies must have constant supervision. Special care must go into their feeding, socialization, and training to assure a happy and healthy dog. Playing is also a pivotal part of puppyhood.

That Bites!

Beagle puppy

Have you ever wondered why your puppy chews on your stuff? The pup chews on hard objects to help its teeth grow in, and they will practice on whatever they can get their teeth on.

Rhodesian
Ridgeback
puppies

American
Staffordshire
Terrier

Puppy Talk

Though puppies may start to have human contact as young as three weeks old, they should stay with their mother for at least seven weeks.

Sleepy Heads

For the first week of their lives, puppies will do nothing but eat and sleep. Up to the age of three months, puppies will go through long sessions of deep sleep.

Golden Retriever puppies

A Dog of My Own

People who want to adopt a dog have many choices. They may buy a purebred dog from a breeder who carefully chose the dog's parents. Or they might adopt a homeless dog from a humane society or rescue organization. The important thing is to find the dog that is right for you and your family. People choosing a dog should look for those who seem happy, energetic, and healthy.

Teacher's Pet

Experts say that every dog should learn to obey five basic commands: sit, down, stay, come, and drop it. Dogs should be praised with treats and love when they respond properly.

On Call

Dogs need regular visits to the doctor—just like people! Dogs should be vaccinated against common illnesses and receive booster shots every year.

Cavalier King Charles Spaniel

CHOW TiMe

English Bulldog

Like humans, dogs need to eat the right foods and drink plenty of water. Dogs love to gnaw on bones, but not all bones are healthy. Never give a dog bones that can splinter, such as turkey or pork bones—they can do serious damage if swallowed.

GLOSSARY

Aggressive: Likely to attack; prepared to be combative.

Agility: A competition at a dog show where dogs follow their owner's commands to race through a timed obstacle course.

Aztec: The Native American tribe dominant in Mexico before the Spanish conquest in the 16th century.

Cairn Terrier: A breed named for its ability to flush out small animals from cairns, small piles of stones that the Scots used to mark memorials or boundaries.

Canid: A family of carnivorous animals that includes wolves, jackals, foxes, coyotes, and domestic dogs.

Canines: Members of the Canidae family. See canid.

Cave canem: Latin words that mean "beware the dog."

Coarse: Rough.

Coat: The external hair or fur on a dog.

Commands: Actions that people teach dogs to perform. Experts say that dogs should learn the commands for sit, down, stay, come, and drop it.

Companionship: The feeling of friendship. Dogs are very loyal and make good companions.

Docile: Obedient; easy to manage.

Dog breeds: Groups of closely related and visibly similar-looking domestic dogs.

Dog fighting: A contest between two dogs bred and trained to fight.

Dog training: Teaching a dog to perform certain actions in response to certain commands that the dog is trained to understand.

Domestic: An animal that is used to living with humans; tame.

Ferret: To search tenaciously.

Flush: To force or drive into the open.

Game: Wild animals or birds, hunted for food or sport.

Gnaw: To bite or chew on, again and again. Puppies go through a stage of gnawing on almost everything.

Humane society: An organization devoted to the promotion of humane ideals, especially in dealing with animals. Some humane societies provide adoption, outreach, training, and humane investigations.

Mongrel: Also called a mutt; a dog that is a mix of two or more breeds.

Nip: To bite or pinch.

Papillon: The terms comes from French, meaning "butterfly."

Puppy: A baby dog. Puppies, like babies, need constant supervision, including special care with their feeding and socialization.

Purebred: An animal whose ancestors are all of the same breed.

Scurry: To move quickly or in a hurried way.

Sled dogs: Dogs trained to pull a dogsled. Siberian Huskies are commonly trained to be sled dogs.

Socialization: The process by which a puppy learns how to get along with other dogs.

Stamina: Endurance.

Submission: The act of surrendering or giving in.

Temperament: A dog's general demeanor or way of responding.

Tenacity: Determination.

Toy breed: A dog of a very small breed or of a variety smaller than the standard of its breed. The very smallest toy dogs are sometimes called teacup size.

Trait: A characteristic or quality that distinguishes one animal from another.

Working breed: Group of dogs bred to perform such jobs as guarding property, pulling sleds, and performing water rescues.